Unlock a world of magic, wonder, and mystery in this unique collection of coloring pages from illustrator R.J. Hampson. Every page tells a story and each whimsical illustration invites the colorist to discover something new as they get lost in the detail, humour, and joy of coloring.

This book contains 25 original hand-drawn illustrations for you to color.

For artists, coloring enthusiasts, and those who are a little lost and long to be found!

See more at rjhampson.com

 russelljamesart

Published by Hop Skip Jump
PO Box 1324 Buderim Queensland Australia 4556

First published 2023.
Copyright © 2023 R.J. Hampson.

All Rights Reserved. Without limiting the rights under copyright reserved above, no part of this publication may be reproduced, stored in or introduced into a retrieval system, or transmitted, in any form or by any means (electronic, mechanical, photocopying, recording or otherwise), without the prior written permission of both the copyright owner and the above publisher of this book. The only exception is by a reviewer who may share short excerpts in a review.

ISBN: 978-1-922472-18-2

FIND A KEY ON EVERY PAGE

Using this book

Find a quiet place away from distractions. Relax and immerse yourself in the process of coloring as you explore the details of each illustration.

This book is best suited to color pencils or markers. Wet mediums should be used sparingly. Slide a card or sheets of paper behind the illustration you are coloring to avoid marker bleed through.

Find fresh coloring pages by signing up to Russell's newsletter. Get free downloadable pages and updates on new books at -

rjhampson.com

PARADISE LOST

LOST IN SPACE

THE KEY TO MY HEART

THE RESCUE

TIME AFTER TIME

THE SEARCH FOR LOST TREASURE

THE LOST LIGHTHOUSE

HELP

LOST IN THE CITY

WITH ALL MY HEART

HOME FOR LOST CATS

OPPOSITES ATTRACT

WRONG TURN

LOST KINGDOM

THE LOST & FOUND

LOST IN WONDER

LOST IN WONDER

LAND OF LOST SOCKS

DESTINY

THE BUG CATCHER

FREEDOM FOUND

FREEDOM FOUND

HIDE & SEEK

THREE WISHES

THE COLLECTOR

PARADISE FOUND

Unlock a world of magic, wonder and mystery!

Find new coloring pages by signing up to R.J. Hampson's newsletter.
Get free downloadable pages, monthly coloring sheets,
and updates on new books at -

rjhampson.com/coloring

Thanks for choosing this coloring book.
If you enjoyed it, please consider leaving a review.
It will help to let more people in on the experience
plus you'd certainly make this illustrator very happy!

Published books in this series

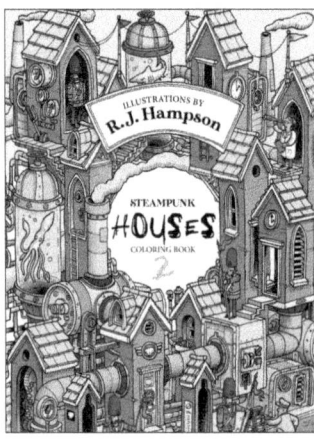

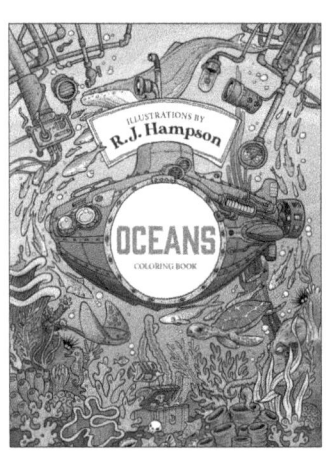

See flip-throughs and new releases at **rjhampson.com**

www.ingramcontent.com/pod-product-compliance
Lightning Source LLC
Chambersburg PA
CBHW041221240426
43661CB00012B/1107